THE BOAT STAR

The Boat Star is a therapeutic story about dealing with a painful loss and taking comfort in good memories. In this poignant story, a boy loses a special feather and goes on a magical journey to try to recover it. Although he doesn't find his feather, he is comforted by the memory of the feather and realises he will feel better over time. This beautifully illustrated storybook will appeal to all children, and can be used by practitioners, educators and parents as a tool to discuss bereavement and coming to terms with feelings of loss with children.

Juliette Ttofa is a Specialist Senior Educational Psychologist with 15 years' experience working with children and young people. She specialises in supporting resilience and well-being in vulnerable children.

Julia Gallego is a picture book illustrator and designer, and a graduate of the Manchester School of Art.

The Boat Star

A Story About Loss

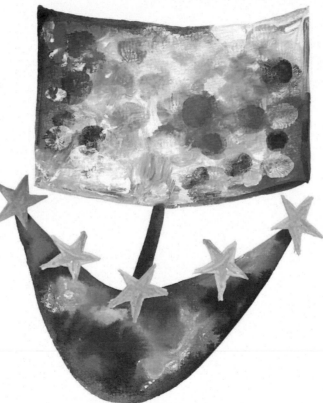

Juliette Ttofa

Illustrated by Julia Gallego

Routledge
Taylor & Francis Group

LONDON AND NEW YORK

First published 2018
by Routledge
2 Park Square, Milton Park, Abingdon, Oxon OX14 4RN

and by Routledge
711 Third Avenue, New York, NY 10017

Routledge is an imprint of the Taylor & Francis Group, an informa business

© 2018 Juliette Ttofa

Illustrations © 2018 Julia Gallego

British Library Cataloguing-in-Publication Data
A catalogue record for this book is available from the British Library

Library of Congress Cataloging-in-Publication Data
A catalog record for this book has been requested

ISBN: 978-1-138-30882-4 (pbk)
ISBN: 978-1-315-14316-3 (ebk)

Typeset in Calibri
by Apex CoVantage, LLC

For Luca
x

There was once a young boy who found a feather by the sea
– a beautiful, long, white feather.
To him, it was unique and special,
and he loved it so.

He held the feather in his hand, soft and warm;
it made him feel loved and he stored the love in his heart.

1

But a cruel wind came and snatched the feather from his hand.

It slipped through his fingers and soared up, up and away, until it was nowhere to be seen.

The boy searched high and low for the feather in disbelief, but despite his efforts he could not bring his feather back.

So he cried and cried, until his eyes ran dry.

3

At night, the little boy would go to sleep dreaming about the white feather.
He longed to see it again. Looking through his window at the night sky,
he wished so much he could hold his feather again.

And though days and weeks
passed, he never
forgot his lost
feather.

One evening, the little boy awoke in his bedroom and made out a strange misty glow in front of him. It was a boat floating on the air!

At the back of the boat was a beautiful net woven from silver and gold.

The boy rubbed his sleepy eyes and sat up.

"Hello!" came some friendly voices, and up popped three little children, each holding a fishing rod.

"We are Winkin, Blinkin and Nod and this is the Boat Star!" exclaimed the three children, who were dressed in their pyjamas.

"We sail the starry seas in the sky and fish for herring-fish and lost things. Will you come with us tonight?" The three children held out a spare fishing rod to the little boy.

The boy thought about this. And he came up with an idea, "Maybe I could ask these children to help me."

So he replied, "If I come with you, will you please help me to find my lost feather? It's white and soft, and I lost it one day."

"White and soft you say?" echoed Winkin, Blinkin and Nod. "Well we need to go to Nimbus then!"

"Nimbus?" asked the little boy.

"The Land of Nimbus!" declared the three curious children. "It is big and soft and white and there are lots of lost things there!"

"Hop in!" beckoned Winkin with a friendly smile.

"Climb aboard!" welcomed Blinkin, with her hand outstretched.

"Let's go!" bellowed Nod.

So the boy said,
"I am ready!"

And taking hold
of his fishing rod,

he caught a ride
with the Boat Star.

Winkin, Blinkin and Nod lit a lantern
on the front of the boat, weighed anchor and
cast the boat loose from its moorings.

Up they went.

The Boat Star soared beyond mackerel skies,
above the Earth, passed the lustrous white
Moon, and high into Space.

As they sailed
through the watery
kingdom high up in the
heavens, they trailed their
silvery-gold net behind them trawling for lost things.

They cruised past Pisces, The Fish – two stars made up of Venus and her son Cupid.

After that, they glided past Dorado, The Goldfish, flashing gold, blue and green as it darted through the sky.

Winkin, Blinkin and Nod showed the boy how they threw bait into the sea – tiny morsels scattering in the sky like a Meteor shower.

The Crab floated by the Boat Star, nipping at the bait and pinching cheekily at their fishing rods.

The little boy couldn't believe his eyes when a playful fish-goat called Capricornus swam by, with the head of a goat and the long, sweeping tail of a fish!

Then, the boy saw the most beautiful sight of all – Delphinus, The Dolphin, dipping and diving, playing and splashing in the waves.

The Dolphin followed the Boat Star, leaping eagerly in its wake.

Winkin, Blinkin and Nod even let the young boy sail the Boat Star all by himself. They all giggled as he zig-zagged from star to star, as if the sky was a giant dot-to-dot picture.

Until finally, they arrived at the Land of Nimbus:
a colossal, white cloud in the blackest blanket of sky.

And in the middle there was a bright, White Hole with
objects and light pouring out of it and other people in boats
all crowded around
its opening.

"This is where all the stuff that gets
sucked into Black Holes comes out!"
called Winkin, Blinkin and Nod.

They dropped anchor, cast out their nets over the entrance to the White Hole and flung their fishing lines far out.

As the lines unravelled, all sorts of objects came spewing out of the White Hole – all manner of lost things like odd socks, coins, sweet wrappers, paper clips and leaky pens.

They all laughed when Nod netted an old shoe. And Blinkin reeled in some reading glasses and a watch. Then Winkin caught a small Asteroid which pulled him whizzing through the air like a firework, until he managed to release it and land back in the Boat Star.

But the boy caught no white feather.

They all checked their nets over and over again, pulled up their fishing lines, but no feather was ever found.

The boy threw down his fishing rod in anger.

All he had to show for his night's fishing
was the memory of the feather, not the real white feather
– not his actual real life, beloved feather.

All of a sudden, the other crowds that had been fishing started to turn around and sail away in a panic.

They looked up and saw the giant Sea Monster, Cetus, heading their way.

"Quick!!" shouted Winkin, Blinkin and Nod. "Hoist up the sail and bring in the nets! We need to get away quickly!"

The boy helped to hoist the main sail, which towered above the Boat Star, rippling with ribbons of colour like the Aurora Borealis,
the Northern Lights.

They sailed fast, but Cetus was catching up with them. There was a storm brewing on the sea and the waves were lashing all around the little Boat Star, tossing it wildly like a toy boat in a bath.

"Hurry!" called Nod. "Head towards the River! Cetus won't be able to swim after us down there and we will be sheltered."

The Boat Star shot past Aquarius, The Water-Bearer, who poured out some golden nectar from his jug to speed the Boat Star's voyage and sweeten their distress.

Finally, they steered into the winding Eridemus River,
where they were safe at last.

As they navigated these calm, crystal-lit waters
the children all sat down in relief.

And the little boy started to cry.

He had come all this way, but he
still hadn't found his lost feather.

Winkin, Blinkin and Nod
hugged the sad little boy.

But as the boy wiped his eyes, he spied something – it was a feather, slicing the wind like a wand.

He grabbed it with excitement . . .

He held the feather in his hand, soft and warm; it made him feel loved and he stored the love in his heart.

But this wasn't his white feather.

"It is too small and it's *gold*," he thought, looking carefully at it, disappointed once again. "Where has it come from?"

Then he noticed rain falling. He gently caught a drop in the palm of his hand and, glancing upwards to see where it had descended from, the boy caught sight of something flying alongside them crying.

23

"What is that amazing creature?" asked
the boy in wonder.

"That is the Phoenix. It is crying because its Father has died.

But legend has it that when the Father Phoenix dies, a little Phoenix is re-born."

The boy held on tightly to the small, gold feather and thought about
this for a while.

The boy was suddenly very tired. As the Phoenix flew off into the distance, he curled up and lay down in the Boat Star.

Winkin, Blinkin and Nod covered their new friend with a soft blanket and before he knew it, he had been lulled into a deep sleep by the rocking motion of the boat, sailing through the stars.

When the boy next awoke, he was back in his bedroom at home and the sun was streaming in through the curtains.

The boy got up and looked out of the window.

Something was tugging at him, a thought or memory that had slipped like quicksilver from his mind.

Then he remembered his dream about the Boat Star and Winkin, Blinkin and Nod.

He searched frantically for the new feather he had found, but it wasn't in his bed or pyjama pockets. It wasn't anywhere.

So the boy got up and went to school as he did every day.
He sat through every lesson without anyone knowing just what was on his mind.

That night the boy said goodnight to his Mum and went to bed thinking about the strange dream he had had the night before.

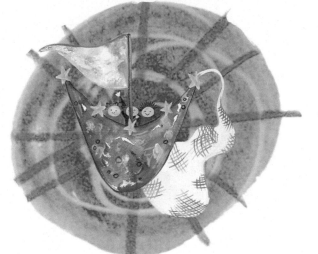

But something was still niggling at him, so he got up and looked out of the window at the stars one last time before bed.

He noticed a star moving slowly through the sky. "Probably a satellite or a space-station" he thought. "But, then again, it looks a bit like the lantern of the Boat Star!"

And he could almost make out the little twinkling figures of Winkin, Blinkin and Nod – three dots – waving to him happily.

Then he recognised the large, bird-shaped constellation in the sky.
"It's the Phoenix!" he smiled.

As he gazed at the gold stars which made up the Phoenix's feathers, it comforted him to know that a Little Phoenix would
be reborn from his Father.

His journey on the Boat Star
had come to an end.
And although he
had not found his
lost feather,

he had found that the memory
of his feather would always live on in him.

It made him feel loved and he stored the love in his heart.

"Maybe a memory can shine as bright as any star,"
he thought as he drifted happily off to sleep with a
wink, a blink and a nod.